I0446138

The Success You Can't See

Unlock the potential of 21 Digital Skills To Earn Money Before the Year Ends

Copyright

All rights reserved. No part of this publication may be reproduced, distributed, or transmitted in any form or by any means, including photocopying, recording, or other electronic or mechanical methods, without the prior written permission of the publisher, except in the case of brief quotations embodied in critical reviews and certain other noncommercial uses permitted by copyright law .

Table of contents

**3
The Success You Can't See**

The Success You Can't See

Introduction:

In today's world, success is often measured by visible accomplishments and traditional paths to success. But there is a realm of achievement that goes unseen. This book is an exploration into the extraordinary potential that can be unlocked with a smartphone.

Success is no longer limited to degrees and wealth. Unconventional avenues are opening up new possibilities for those with the vision to look beyond the ordinary. This book is a testament to the fact that success is not confined to what we can see. It is a journey shaped by the mastery of digital skills and the art of leveraging them through the smartphone.

We will unlock the secrets to building success in ways that may not be immediately apparent. The smartphone is not just a device; it's a portal to a myriad of opportunities. We'll explore how acquiring essential digital skills can transform your smartphone into a powerful tool for financial growth and personal fulfillment.

The stories in this book will challenge conventional notions of success, proving that the journey to prosperity is as diverse as the individuals who embark upon it. We'll navigate the landscape of online entrepreneurship, uncovering business ideas that can be nurtured and developed with nothing more than the device in your hand.

Come with me on this expedition into the unseen, where success is not a destination but a dynamic, ever-evolving journey. By the end of this exploration, you'll understand that the true measure of success lies not just in what you can see, but in the vast realm of possibilities that await those who dare to embrace the unconventional and harness the power of the unseen. Get ready to redefine success on your own terms, armed with nothing more than the success you can't see—yet.

The Success You Can't See

The Power of Digital Skills:

In this day and age of rapid technological progress, digital skills have become the foundation of personal and professional development. This chapter will explore the far-reaching effects of digital skills on our lives, work, and connections.

Digital skills cover a wide range, from basic knowledge of the digital world to advanced abilities in coding, data analysis, and digital marketing. As we traverse this digital age, the capacity to adjust, learn, and use these skills is not only advantageous but, in many cases, essential.

The power of digital skills is most evident in their capacity to democratize knowledge and opportunities. Unlike traditional obstacles that once limited access to certain industries or professions, the digital world provides an open playing field where individuals can educate themselves, link up with global networks, and demonstrate their talents, regardless of geographical boundaries.

Furthermore, digital skills empower people to navigate the intricate landscape of information. In an era characterized by an abundance of data, the ability to discern, interpret, and utilize information has become a skill in itself. Those with digital skills are better equipped to draw meaningful conclusions, make informed decisions, and contribute meaningfully to a knowledge-driven society.

One of the most remarkable transformations brought about by digital skills is the democratization of entrepreneurship. With just a smartphone and the right skill set, individuals can now create and market their products or services globally. The barriers to entry for startups have significantly decreased, allowing creative ideas to thrive and challenge the status quo.

The workplace landscape has also undergone a radical transformation. Digital skills are no longer restricted to IT departments; they have become integral to various industries. Proficiency in tools like project management software, graphic design applications, and data analytics platforms is becoming increasingly necessary for success in diverse professional fields.

In the realm of education, digital skills enable new and dynamic ways of learning. Online courses, virtual classrooms, and interactive platforms provide accessible avenues for individuals to upgrade and re skill, fostering a culture of lifelong learning.

The Success You Can't See

Nevertheless, the transformative impact of digital skills is not without its challenges. As industries evolve and automation becomes more widespread, there is a pressing need for individuals to continuously update their skill sets to stay relevant. Additionally, the digital divide—a gap between those with access to technology and those without—poses difficulties in ensuring that the advantages of digital skills are inclusive and accessible to all.

The Smartphone Revolution

The smartphone revolution has
been a seismic shift in the way we
communicate, work, and live our
daily lives. Smartphones have
become an integral part of our
identities, influencing how we
express ourselves, connect with
others, and consume information.
They are no longer just gadgets;
they are personalized hubs, housing
our preferences, memories, and
aspirations.

The invention of the smartphone is
a testament to human ingenuity,
relentless innovation, and the
desire to reshape the way we
communicate and interact with the
world. The concept of a handheld
device that could do more than just
make calls began to take shape in
the late 20th century. In 1992, IBM
introduced the Simon Personal
Communicator, often considered
the first true smartphone.

The Success You Can't See

The true explosion of smartphones occurred in the 21st century, driven by companies that would become synonymous with innovation in this space. In 2007, Apple unveiled the first iPhone, a device that redefined the concept of a phone by integrating a full-touchscreen interface, internet capabilities, and an array of applications. The iPhone's impact was revolutionary, setting the standard for smartphones to come.

The evolution of smartphones was marked by significant technological advancements. Improvements in processors, displays, cameras, and connectivity transformed these devices into powerful tools that could handle complex tasks and offer immersive user experiences. The advent of app stores further expanded the functionality of smartphones, allowing users to customize their devices with a vast array of applications.

Smartphones have brought immense convenience and connectivity, but they have also raised concerns such as digital addiction, privacy, and the digital divide. However, they have also presented opportunities for education, entrepreneurship, and empowerment, particularly in regions where traditional infrastructure was lacking.

The smartphone revolution has been a cultural and technological transformation that has reshaped the fabric of societies across the globe. It has redefined how we communicate, work, and navigate our daily lives, and it has opened up a world of possibilities.

The smartphone revolution has opened up a world of possibilities, allowing people to become active participants in the digital economy.

This pocket-sized device has broken down traditional barriers to knowledge and information, giving users the power to learn, explore their interests, and develop skills at their own pace. This democratization of information has created a culture of continuous learning and self-improvement.

The smartphone is more than just a device; it is a tool that can help people to overcome limitations and shape their own destinies. With access to online courses, the ability to network with professionals, and the chance to showcase their talents on digital platforms, the smartphone revolution has made it easier than ever before to pursue success.

The Power of Digital Skills: Unleashing Transformation in the Modern World**

The Success You Can't See

The modern world is being reshaped by digital skills, which have become essential for success in the contemporary landscape. This chapter examines the power of digital skills, exploring how they are enabling profound transformation in how we work, communicate, and navigate the complexities of the digital age.

Digital skills encompass a wide range of proficiencies, from basic computer literacy to advanced capabilities such as programming, data analysis, and digital marketing. The availability of online platforms, courses, and tutorials has made education accessible to a global audience, allowing individuals from diverse backgrounds to acquire skills and expertise. This democratization of knowledge has fostered a culture of continuous learning, where anyone with an internet connection can embark on a journey of self-improvement.

Digital skills also serve as a gateway to entrepreneurship in the digital age. Those with coding abilities can bring software solutions to life, digital marketers can reach global audiences, and e-commerce entrepreneurs can establish online businesses with relative ease. The digital realm has significantly lowered the barriers to entry for aspiring entrepreneurs, providing them with the tools to turn innovative ideas into reality.

The workplace is undergoing a profound transformation, with digital skills at the forefront of this evolution. Proficiency in project management software, data analysis tools, and digital communication platforms is now a fundamental expectation across various industries. The adaptability and versatility of those with robust digital skills make them invaluable contributors to a workforce navigating the complexities of a digitalized world.

Digital skills are also the bedrock of innovation. Those with digital proficiency are at the forefront of driving progress, leveraging digital tools to tackle challenges, explore new possibilities, and contribute to the ongoing evolution of industries.

While the transformative impact of digital skills is profound, it is not without challenges. The rapid pace of technological change demands continuous upskilling and adaptation. Additionally, addressing the digital divide—ensuring that access to digital education and tools is equitable—remains a critical societal concern.

Overview of Digital Skills

In today's digital world, having the right digital skills is not only necessary for navigating the online space but also a great way to make money, especially with the help of a smartphone. These skills range from technical abilities to creative talents, all of which are essential for creating a successful online presence. Here is a look at some of the key digital skills that can be used to monetize a smartphone:

1. **Content Creation:**
  - *Description:* The ability to create interesting and high-quality content, such as written articles, images, or videos, is essential. Content creation is the foundation of digital marketing and can be monetized through various

platforms like social media, blogs, and video-sharing sites.

2. **Social Media Management:**
   - *Description:* Knowing how to manage and optimize social media accounts is essential for individuals and businesses looking to establish a strong online presence. From building a following to implementing marketing strategies, social media management is a key skill for monetizing digital platforms.

3. **Digital Marketing:**
   - *Description:* Understanding the principles of digital marketing, including SEO (Search Engine Optimization), SEM (Search Engine Marketing), and email marketing, is essential. These skills enable individuals to promote products, services, or content effectively and reach a wider audience.

4. **Graphic Design:**

- *Description:* Graphic design skills are necessary for creating visually appealing and professional graphics for marketing materials, social media posts, and websites. There are many apps and tools available for graphic design, making it accessible to smartphone users.

5. **Basic Coding and Web Development:**
   - *Description:* Although not required, having a basic understanding of coding languages (HTML, CSS) and web development allows individuals to customize their online presence. It also facilitates the creation of simple websites or landing pages to showcase products or services.

6. **Video Editing:**
   - *Description:* Video content is a major force in digital marketing. Knowing how to edit videos, add effects, and enhance overall quality is a valuable skill. With

smartphone-friendly editing apps, individuals can create professional-looking videos.

7. **Data Analytics:**
   - *Description:* Analyzing and interpreting data is essential for making informed decisions in the digital realm. Digital entrepreneurs can use analytics tools to understand user behavior, track the performance of their content, and optimize their strategies accordingly.

Skill Development Strategies

Developing digital skills can be done through various strategies, allowing individuals to tailor their learning experiences to their preferences and schedules. Here are some tips for developing essential digital skills for making money with a smartphone:

1. **Online Courses:**
   - *Tip:* Sign up for online courses offered by platforms like Coursera, Udemy, or LinkedIn Learning. These courses cover a wide range of digital skills, providing structured and comprehensive learning experiences.

2. **Mobile Apps:**
   - *Tip:* Use mobile apps designed for skill development. Apps like Skillshare, Duolingo, and Canva offer interactive lessons and

activities, making learning convenient on a smartphone.

3. **Self-Study and Practice:**
   - *Tip:* Take advantage of free online resources and tutorials. Platforms like YouTube and blogs offer a wealth of information on various digital skills. Practicing regularly will help reinforce your understanding.

4. **Networking and Collaboration:**
   - *Tip:* Join online communities related to your chosen digital skills. Participate in discussions, seek advice, and collaborate with others. Networking can provide valuable insights and opportunities for skill enhancement.

5. **Project-Based Learning:**
   - *Tip:* Apply your skills to real-world projects. Whether it's creating a blog, managing social media for a small business, or developing a personal website,

hands-on projects can help improve
practical knowledge.

6. **Continuous Learning:**
  - *Tip:* Digital technologies and
trends evolve quickly. Stay up to
date by following industry blogs,
attending webinars, and
participating in online forums.
Adopting a mindset of continuous
learning is key to staying relevant.

7. **Feedback and Iteration:**
  - *Tip:* Get feedback on your
work from peers, mentors, or
online communities. Constructive
feedback is invaluable for
improvement. Be open to making
changes to your projects based on
the input you receive.

The Only Requirement You Need

Success with digital skills requires a combination of technical proficiency, adaptability, and a strategic mindset. To increase your chances of success, here are 10 requirements to consider:

1. **Technical Proficiency:**
   - *Requirement:* Have a strong foundation in the digital skills relevant to your field. Keep up with the latest tools, software, and technologies to stay competitive.

2. **Continuous Learning Mindset:**
   - *Requirement:* Adopt a mindset of lifelong learning. Make sure to stay informed about industry trends, emerging technologies, and best practices

through courses, workshops, and self-directed learning.

3. **Adaptability and Flexibility:**
   - *Requirement:* The digital world changes quickly. Be able to adjust and be flexible to manage changes, switch strategies, and accept new technologies as they come.

4. **Effective Communication Skills:**
   - *Requirement:* Good communication is essential, whether you're working with a team, freelancing, or dealing with clients. Clear and concise communication helps collaboration and client satisfaction.

5. **Problem-Solving Abilities:**
   - *Requirement:* Develop strong problem-solving skills. The ability to analyze problems, come up with effective solutions, and troubleshoot technical issues is

essential for success in the digital space.

6. **Creativity and Innovation:**
   - *Requirement:* Cultivate creativity to bring innovative solutions. Whether it's designing, coding, or strategizing, a creative approach will make you stand out in the digital realm.

7. **Time Management Skills:**
   - *Requirement:* Efficient time management is key. Managing various tasks, meeting deadlines, and staying productive are important for success in a fast-paced digital environment.

8. **Networking and Relationship Building:**
   - *Requirement:* Build a strong professional network. Networking opens doors to opportunities, collaborations, and industry insights. Establish genuine relationships with peers, mentors, and potential clients.

9. **Business Acumen:**
   - *Requirement:* Understand the business side of your digital skills. Whether you're freelancing or running your own venture, learn the basics of entrepreneurship, marketing, and financial management.

10. **Cybersecurity Awareness:**
    - *Requirement:* In the digital age, protecting information is essential. Be aware of cybersecurity best practices to protect yourself and your clients from potential threats and vulnerabilities.

11. **Digital Marketing Savvy:**
    - *Requirement:* Have a good grasp of the fundamentals of digital marketing. Whether you're a content creator, freelancer, or business owner, being knowledgeable about SEO, social

media marketing, and online advertising can significantly boost your visibility and reach.

12. **Data Analysis and Interpretation Skills:**
   - *Requirement:* Get familiar with data analytics tools. Being able to collect, analyze, and interpret data provides invaluable insights for decision-making, optimization, and recognizing trends.

13. **Project Management Expertise:**
   - *Requirement:* Cultivate project management skills to efficiently plan, execute, and finish digital projects. Whether working alone or in a team, effective project management guarantees tasks are completed on time and within scope.

14. **Customer Service Excellence:**

- *Requirement:* Make customer service a priority. Whether you're dealing with clients, users, or customers, providing excellent service builds trust, fosters positive relationships, and can lead to repeat business or positive referrals.

15. **Emotional Intelligence:**
   - *Requirement:* Enhance your emotional intelligence. Digital collaboration often lacks face-to-face interaction, making emotional intelligence essential for understanding and navigating virtual relationships and team dynamics.

16. **Coding and Programming Proficiency:**
   - *Requirement:* Depending on your field, having a basic understanding of coding and programming can be beneficial. It opens up possibilities for customization, problem-solving, and collaboration with developers.

17. **User Experience (UX) Design Knowledge:**
   - *Requirement:* Get acquainted with UX design principles. Whether you're creating content or developing apps, understanding how users interact with digital interfaces is critical for delivering a positive experience.

18. **Financial Literacy:**
   - *Requirement:* Acquire financial literacy relevant to your field. Understand budgeting, pricing strategies, and financial management to guarantee the profitability and sustainability of your digital ventures.

19. **Legal and Ethical Awareness:**
   - *Requirement:* Stay up to date on legal and ethical considerations in the digital space. This includes issues like copyright, intellectual property, privacy, and compliance with industry regulations.

20. **Self-Promotion and Branding:**
   - *Requirement:* Learn how to effectively promote yourself or your brand. Building a personal brand, showcasing your work, and effectively communicating your value proposition are key to success in the competitive digital landscape.

21. **Global Awareness and Cultural Sensitivity:**
   - *Requirement:* Develop global awareness and cultural sensitivity. In an interconnected world, understanding diverse perspectives and cultural nuances is essential for effective communication and collaboration on a global scale.

Do You Need Any Degree Or Certificate?

No, having a degree is not a must for success in the digital world. This is because the digital landscape values practical skills, experience, and demonstrated capabilities more than traditional academic credentials. Here are some reasons why someone may not need a degree to succeed with digital skills:

1. **Skill-Based Industry:**
   - Digital skills are often skill-based, meaning employers and clients are more interested in what you can do rather than the degrees you hold. A strong portfolio and real-world projects can be more impressive than academic qualifications.

2. **Rapidly Changing Technologies:**

- The digital industry is constantly evolving, and traditional education systems may not be able to keep up with the latest trends and technologies. Self-taught individuals or those who engage in continuous learning can adapt more quickly to changes.

3. **Online Learning Resources:**
   - There are plenty of online resources, including tutorials, courses, and certifications, that allow individuals to acquire digital skills independently. Platforms like Coursera, Udemy, and others provide accessible and affordable learning opportunities.

4. **Freelancing and Entrepreneurship:**
   - Many successful individuals in the digital space are freelancers or entrepreneurs who have built their careers based on practical skills and real-world experience. Clients and customers often prioritize

results over academic
qualifications.

5. **Portfolio and Experience:**
   - Building a strong portfolio that
showcases your work and practical
applications of your skills can be
more compelling to potential
employers or clients than a degree.
Practical experience and tangible
results often carry significant
weight.

6. **Networking and
Connections:**
   - Networking and building
connections within the industry can
play a crucial role in success.
Personal connections,
recommendations, and a strong
professional network can open
doors and create opportunities,
regardless of formal education.

7. **Specialized Certifications:**
   - Specific certifications relevant
to certain digital skills can
sometimes be more valuable than a

general degree. Certifications demonstrate a focused expertise in a particular area and can be obtained through targeted training programs.

8. **Entrepreneurial Spirit:**
   - The digital space often rewards entrepreneurial spirit and creativity. Individuals who can identify opportunities, innovate, and create value are highly sought after, and these traits are not necessarily dependent on formal education.

9. **Portfolio Showcase:**
   - A strong and diverse portfolio is a powerful tool for showcasing your skills and accomplishments. Employers and clients often value tangible evidence of your abilities, such as completed projects, more than academic credentials.

10. **Self-Directed Learning:**
   - The ability to learn independently and self-direct your

education is highly valued in the digital space. Many successful professionals in the field are self-taught individuals who have honed their skills through online resources and practical applications.

Success in the digital world without a degree is achievable with the right combination of skills, learning, self-promotion, and engagement in the industry. While a degree may be beneficial in some cases, the digital space offers many alternative routes for individuals to succeed based on their abilities and contributions. Open source contributions, building a personal brand, project-based learning, freelance platforms and gig economy, industry certifications and bootcamps, demonstrated problem-solving, internships and apprenticeships, soft skills development, online presence and networking, and feedback and iteration are all important elements to consider.

These elements can help you to establish yourself as an authority in your field, gain valuable hands-on experience, and develop the skills needed to collaborate effectively in a digital work environment. Ultimately, these are the key ingredients to success in the digital world without a degree.

What is the age limit?

There is no age limit when it comes to learning and developing digital skills. The digital world is open to everyone, regardless of age, who is willing to explore and acquire new knowledge. Here are some key points to consider:

The Success You Can't See

1. **Flexible Learning Platforms:**
   - Digital skills can be learned through a variety of online platforms, courses, and resources. Many of these resources are tailored to different learning styles and paces, making them accessible to people of all ages.

2. **Continuous Learning:**
   - The digital world is constantly changing, and continuous learning is a part of the culture. It doesn't matter how old you are, the ability to adapt and embrace new technologies and concepts is more important than any specific starting age.

3. **Career Transitions:**
   - Many people choose to learn digital skills later in life as part of a career transition. It's not uncommon for people in their 30s, 40s, or even later to acquire digital skills and transition into tech-related careers successfully.

4. **Entrepreneurial Opportunities:**
  - Digital skills can empower individuals to start their own businesses or pursue entrepreneurial ventures. Age is not a barrier to entrepreneurship, and many successful digital entrepreneurs have started later in life.

5. **Community Support:**
  - Online communities and forums provide support and encouragement for learners of all ages. Whether you're a teenager or in your retirement years, there are communities where individuals share their learning journeys and provide assistance.

6. **Personalized Learning Paths:**
  - Learning paths can be tailored to individual preferences and goals. Whether you're interested in web development, digital marketing,

data science, or other fields, you can choose a path that aligns with your interests and career objectives.

7. **Mentorship:**
   - Mentorship is invaluable in the digital space. People of any age can benefit from the guidance and insights of mentors who have experience in the field.

8. **In-Demand Skills:**
   - Digital skills are in high demand across various industries. Regardless of your age, acquiring these skills can enhance your professional profile and open up new opportunities in the job market.

9. **Personal Growth and Hobbies:**
   - Learning digital skills can also be pursued as a personal interest or hobby. Whether you're a student, working professional, or someone in retirement, the pursuit of

knowledge and personal growth is a rewarding endeavor.

10. **Lifelong Learning:**
   - Adopting a lifelong learning philosophy is beneficial at any age. The ability to stay curious, adapt to change, and acquire new skills is a mindset that is not limited by age.

The digital world is an incredibly vast and inclusive space, open to people of all ages. Whether you're a teenager looking to learn coding or a retiree wanting to start an online business, there are plenty of opportunities to explore and develop digital skills. Digital skills can be used to reinvent careers, work remotely, make a positive impact on society, collaborate with people from different generations, and access educational resources.

There are also initiatives to help seniors become digitally literate, as well as creative outlets for individuals to express themselves.

Learning digital skills can be a family affair, and it can also be a great way to connect with people from all over the world.

Plus, many local communities offer digital literacy programs and workshops to bridge the digital divide. All in all, the digital world is a place where everyone can learn, grow, and make a difference.

Introduction to Money-Making Business Ideas

The Digital Revolution:
The internet and digital technologies have revolutionized the way we communicate and access information, and have opened up countless opportunities for people to make money from their digital skills. Now, individuals with a variety of skills and talents

can use the digital world to create successful businesses and generate income with minimal upfront costs.

Unlocking the Power of Digital Skills:
Digital skills, such as content creation, social media management, coding, and digital marketing, are now essential for success in the digital economy. These skills provide the foundation for various money-making opportunities, allowing people to monetize their expertise and creativity.

Diverse Avenues for Income Generation:
The possibilities for turning digital skills into money-making ventures are vast and varied. From freelance work and online entrepreneurship to affiliate marketing and e-commerce, individuals can choose from a range of options that suit their skills, interests, and goals. The digital landscape is a

playground for innovation, offering the flexibility to explore unconventional and niche business ideas.

The Rise of Remote Work:
The shift towards remote work and the gig economy has further increased the potential for money-making opportunities. Professionals and freelancers can now collaborate with clients and businesses from all over the world, eliminating geographical barriers and expanding the reach of their services. This has changed the way we think about work, and digital skills are now highly sought after and valued.

Tailoring Digital Skills to Market Needs:
Success in the digital marketplace depends on the ability to identify and meet market needs. Entrepreneurs who understand how to effectively market their skills and offerings can create products

or services that are in demand, and establish themselves as authorities in their respective niches. The key is to align digital skills with market demands and stay up to date with the latest trends.

The Journey Ahead:
As we explore the various money-making business ideas, it's important to remember that the digital landscape is constantly changing. The following sections will look at specific ways individuals can use their digital skills to create profitable ventures. From e-commerce and affiliate marketing to online entrepreneurship, there are plenty of opportunities for those willing to take the plunge and turn their digital prowess into a sustainable and rewarding source of income.

21 Simple Digital Skills That Require Only Your Smartphone

1. Social media manager

Introduction:
Being a successful social media manager requires more than just posting content; it takes a strategic and creative approach to engage audiences effectively. Here are some tips to help you thrive in this dynamic role:

a. Stay Up-to-Date and Flexible:
   - Keep up with the latest trends and updates in social media platforms.
   - Be prepared to adjust to changes in algorithms and user behavior.

b. Know Your Audience:
   - Do thorough research on your target demographic to tailor content to them.

- Interact with your audience through comments, messages, and polls to understand their preferences.

c. Create a Content Plan:
- Plan and schedule content in advance to maintain consistency.
- Mix up the types of content you post, such as images, videos, and text, to keep the feed interesting.

d. Use Analytics:
- Regularly analyze the performance of your posts.
- Use the insights to refine your strategy, focusing on content that resonates with your audience.

e. Foster Engagement:
- Build a sense of community by responding to comments and messages.
- Encourage user-generated content to increase community participation.

f. Be Creative:

- Experiment with different formats and storytelling techniques.
- Utilize visuals, such as infographics and eye-catching graphics, to grab attention.

g. Collaborate and Network:
- Work with influencers and other brands to expand your reach.
- Attend industry events and connect with other social media professionals.

h. Stay Ethical and Genuine:
- Be transparent and authentic in your communication.
- Follow ethical guidelines when promoting products or services.

i. Keep Up with Trends:
- Embrace emerging trends and incorporate them into your strategy.
- Take advantage of new features introduced by social media platforms to stay ahead.

j. Measure ROI:

- Set clear goals and metrics to measure the return on investment (ROI).
- Use data to show the impact of your social media efforts on the overall business objectives.

Introduction:
Making money from selling unwanted products can be a great way to make some extra cash. Here are some tips to help you make the process easier and more successful:

a. Quality Imagery:
- Take clear, high-quality photos of your items from different angles.
- Showcase any special or valuable features.

b. Accurate Descriptions:
- Provide detailed and honest descriptions of your items.
- Don't forget to mention any flaws or imperfections to build trust with potential buyers.

c. Pricing Strategy:
   - Do some research to set a competitive yet reasonable price for your items.
   - Consider offering bundle deals or discounts for multiple items.

d. Choose the Right Platform:
   - Select a platform that aligns with your target audience.
   - Platforms like eBay, Facebook Marketplace, or specialized apps cater to different markets.

e. Prompt Communication:
   - Reply to inquiries quickly and professionally.
   - Be ready to negotiate but know your bottom line.

f. Safe and Secure Transactions:
   - Safety should be your top priority; meet in public places for exchanges.

- For online transactions, use secure payment methods to avoid scams.

g. Utilize Social Media:
- Use your social media networks to promote your items.
- Share posts with friends and ask for referrals.

h. Update Listings Regularly:
- Keep your listings up-to-date by removing sold items promptly.
- Refresh your listings periodically to attract new buyers.

i. Provide Excellent Customer Service:
- Give clear shipping information.
- Communicate proactively with buyers to ensure a positive experience.

j. Consider Shipping Options:
- Look into shipping options to reach a wider audience.

- Remember to factor shipping costs into your pricing strategy.

Introduction:
Sharing your knowledge and making money at the same time is possible with how-to videos on YouTube. Here are some tips to help you monetize your knowledge effectively:

a. Identify Your Niche:
- Pick a topic or niche that is related to your expertise.
- Make sure your content stands out from the rest in the same niche.

b. Engaging Thumbnails and Titles:
- Create eye-catching thumbnails and titles to draw in viewers.
- Make sure your titles and thumbnails clearly explain the value of your video.

c. Quality Content Production:

- Invest in good video and audio equipment for a professional-looking production.
- Edit your videos carefully to keep viewers engaged.

d. Consistent Upload Schedule:
- Establish a consistent uploading schedule to build an audience.
- Regular uploads will help you become more visible on the platform.

e. SEO Optimization:
- Research keywords related to your content and include them in your video titles, descriptions, and tags.
- Utilize YouTube analytics to refine your SEO strategy.

f. Create Series and Playlists:
- Develop video series to encourage viewers to watch multiple videos.
- Organize your content into playlists for easy navigation.

g. Audience Interaction:
   - Respond to comments and engage with your audience.
   - Encourage viewers to subscribe, like, and share your videos.

h. Monetization Features:
   - Qualify for YouTube's Partner Program to enable monetization.
   - Explore additional revenue streams, such as channel memberships and merchandise shelves.

i. Collaborate with Others:
   - Collaborate with other YouTubers in your niche to expand your audience.
   - Participate in community events and shout-outs to cross-promote.

j. Diversify Income Streams:
   - Explore affiliate marketing by promoting relevant products in your videos.
   - Consider creating exclusive content for platforms like Patreon

to provide additional value for your supporters.

Introduction:
Selling pre-owned or handmade items can be a great way to make some extra money and declutter. To ensure a successful selling experience, here are some tips to keep in mind:

a. Clean and Present Your Items Well:
   - Make sure to clean and polish your items before listing them.
   - Take clear and high-quality photos from different angles.

b. Provide Accurate Descriptions:
   - Be honest about the condition of your items.
   - Clearly describe any wear, damage, or imperfections.

c. Set Realistic Prices:

- Do your research to set fair and competitive prices.
- Consider the age and condition of the item when pricing.

d. Choose the Right Platform:
- Select platforms that are suitable for the type of items you're selling.
- Utilize popular online marketplaces or dedicated apps.

e. Be Responsive and Professional:
- Reply to inquiries from potential buyers in a timely manner.
- Maintain professionalism in all communication.

f. Negotiate Thoughtfully:
- Be open to negotiation, but know your bottom line.
- Clearly communicate any non-negotiable terms.

g. Provide Secure Transaction Options:

- Choose safe and secure payment methods.
- For in-person transactions, meet in public places during daylight hours.

h. Utilize Social Media:
- Use your social media networks to reach a wider audience.
- Share your listings with friends and ask for referrals.

i. Update Listings Regularly:
- Keep your listings up-to-date by marking items as sold.
- Refresh your listings periodically to maintain visibility.

j. Consider Bundle Deals:
- Offer bundle deals for related items.
- This can encourage buyers to purchase multiple items from you.

Introduction:

Paid surveys offer a convenient way to make some extra money. To make the most of this opportunity, consider the following tips:

a. Choose Reliable Survey Sites:
   - Do your research and select trustworthy survey websites.
   - Read reviews and testimonials to make sure they are reliable.

b. Set Up a Dedicated Email:
   - Use a separate email address for survey invitations.
   - This will help you keep track of survey-related correspondence.

c. Be Honest and Accurate:
   - Provide truthful and accurate information in your survey responses.
   - Consistent and honest answers will increase your credibility.

d. Fill Out Profiles Thoroughly:

- Complete your profile on survey platforms completely.
- This will ensure you get surveys that match your demographics.

e. Respond Quickly:
- Complete surveys as soon as you receive invitations.
- Some surveys have limited slots, so acting fast increases your chances.

f. Set Reasonable Expectations:
- Understand that income from paid surveys may be supplemental.
- Set realistic expectations regarding the frequency and payout of surveys.

g. Try Multiple Platforms:
- Sign up for multiple survey platforms to access a variety of opportunities.
- Diversifying your survey sources can increase potential earnings.

h. Redeem Rewards Wisely:
- Familiarize yourself with the redemption options offered by survey sites.
- Choose rewards that align with your preferences or needs.

i. Stay Consistent:
- Regularly check your survey accounts for new opportunities.
- Consistency in participation increases your chances of qualifying for high-paying surveys.

j. Protect Your Privacy:
- Be careful about sharing sensitive information.
- Only provide information necessary for survey participation.

Introduction:
Being a successful video editor requires a combination of technical skills and creative vision. To excel in this field, consider the following tips:

a. Get Familiar with Editing Software:
   - Choose a professional video editing software (e.g., Adobe Premiere Pro, Final Cut Pro, DaVinci Resolve).
   - Take the time to learn its features and functionalities thoroughly.

b. Create a Unique Style:
   - Develop a distinctive editing style that sets you apart.
   - Try out different techniques and effects to refine your signature style.

c. Understand Storytelling:
   - Grasp the basics of storytelling and how it translates to visual narratives.
   - Edit with the audience's emotional engagement in mind.

d. Focus on Sound Design:
   - Acknowledge the importance of sound in video editing.

- Master audio editing techniques for clear, crisp, and immersive sound.

e. Streamline Your Workflow:
- Establish an efficient workflow to maximize productivity.
- Organize project files, use keyboard shortcuts, and optimize rendering settings.

f. Stay Informed of Trends:
- Keep up with industry trends and emerging editing techniques.
- Incorporate relevant trends into your work to stay current.

g. Pay Attention to Detail:
- Pay close attention to details such as transitions, color grading, and pacing.
- Small nuances can have a big impact on the overall quality of the video.

h. Collaborate and Get Feedback:

- Work with other content creators and learn from their experiences.
- Seek constructive feedback to continually improve your skills.

i. Optimize for Different Platforms:
- Understand the specifications and requirements of different platforms.
- Optimize your videos for various resolutions, aspect ratios, and formats.

j. Build a Solid Portfolio:
- Put together a portfolio featuring your best work.
- Showcase your versatility by including a wide range of projects.

11. Strategies for Successful Content Creation:

Introduction:

Content creation is a broad field, encompassing writing, visuals, audio, and more. To excel in this dynamic area, consider the following strategies:

a. Know Your Audience:
  - Clearly define who you are creating content for.
  - Design your content to appeal to their interests and preferences.

b. Quality Matters:
  - Focus on delivering quality content over quantity.
  - Make sure your content is valuable to your audience.

c. Variety is Key:
  - Experiment with different content formats (e.g., blog posts, videos, podcasts).
  - Accommodate different audience preferences and consumption habits.

d. Master Storytelling:

- Become an expert in storytelling.
- Create narratives that captivate and engage your audience emotionally.

e. Incorporate Visuals:
- Incorporate visuals into your content.
- Use high-quality images, infographics, and other visuals to enhance understanding.

f. Utilize SEO:
- Implement SEO best practices to improve discoverability.
- Do keyword research to optimize your content for search engines.

g. Connect with Your Audience:
- Foster a sense of community by engaging with your audience.
- Respond to comments, messages, and social media interactions.

h. Establish Brand Identity:
  - Establish a consistent brand identity across all your content.
  - Use a unified color scheme, logo, and tone of voice.

i. Stay Informed:
  - Stay up-to-date on industry trends and evolving content formats.
  - Embrace new tools and technologies to enhance your content creation capabilities.

j. Analyze Performance:
  - Utilize analytics tools to understand the performance of your content.
  - Analyze metrics such as engagement, click-through rates, and conversion rates.

Introduction:
Creating and selling ebooks is a great way to share knowledge and make passive income. To be

successful in this venture, here are some tips to keep in mind:

a. Pick a Niche:
 - Choose a topic that you are passionate about.
 - Do some research to make sure there is a demand for your chosen niche.

b. Create Quality Content:
 - Put together well-researched and engaging content.
 - Take the time to write, edit, and format your ebook to make it look professional.

c. Design an Appealing Cover:
 - Create an eye-catching cover for your ebook.
 - The cover is the first thing people will see and it can be a deciding factor in whether they buy it or not.

d. Optimize Formatting:

- Format your ebook to be compatible with different devices (e.g., Kindle, Nook, PDF).
- Make sure the reading experience is smooth across all platforms.

e. Use Marketing Strategies:
- Plan out your marketing strategy before launching your ebook.
- Utilize social media, email marketing, and other channels to get the word out.

f. Set a Reasonable Price:
- Look into pricing strategies for ebooks in your genre.
- Offer promotional prices or discounts during launch.

g. Get Reviews and Testimonials:
- Ask early readers to leave reviews.
- Positive reviews will help build your ebook's credibility and visibility.

h. Look into Self-Publishing Platforms:

- Use self-publishing platforms like Amazon Kindle Direct Publishing (KDP) or other ebook distribution platforms.

- Make sure you understand the platform's guidelines and terms.

i. Create a Series or Sequels:

- Think about creating a series of ebooks.

- This can help you get repeat readers and increase sales.

j. Connect with Your Audience:

- Reach out to your readers through social media or a website.

- Listen to their feedback and use it to make your future ebooks even better.

Introduction:

The Success You Can't See

Being a successful podcast host requires a combination of passion, expertise, and strategy. To make your podcast stand out, consider the following tips:

a. Identify Your Niche and Audience:
   - Choose a topic that you are passionate about and knowledgeable about.
   - Get to know your target audience so you can tailor your content to their interests.

b. Invest in Quality Equipment:
   - Invest in a good microphone, headphones, and recording/editing software.
   - High-quality audio is essential for keeping listeners engaged.

c. Plan Engaging Content:
   - Create a content plan with well-structured episodes.

- Mix up the format of your episodes with interviews, storytelling, and discussions.

d. Set a Consistent Release Schedule:
   - Establish a regular release schedule for your episodes.
   - Consistency builds trust and anticipation from your audience.

e. Optimize for Search Engines:
   - Utilize SEO strategies for podcast titles, descriptions, and episode titles.
   - This will help your podcast be more discoverable on podcast platforms.

f. Create Eye-Catching Artwork:
   - Design visually appealing podcast artwork.
   - Your artwork is the first thing potential listeners will see, so make it memorable.

**g. Engage with Your
Listeners:**
- Foster a sense of community by
encouraging listener interaction.
- Respond to comments,
messages, and feedback.

h. Leverage Social Media:
- Utilize social media platforms
to promote your podcast.
- Share behind-the-scenes content
and engage with your audience.

**i. Collaborate with Other
Podcasters:**
- Collaborate with other
podcasters in your niche.
- Cross-promotion can introduce
your podcast to new listeners.

**j. Monitor Analytics and
Adjust:**
- Track analytics to understand
listener demographics and
behaviors.
- Use insights to refine your
content and promotional strategies.

17. Strategies for Achieving Success in Online Gaming and eSports:

Introduction:
Online gaming and eSports have become incredibly competitive. To make it to the top, here are some strategies to consider:

a. Master Your Chosen Game:
  - Spend time honing your skills in the game you want to compete in.
  - Keep up with the latest patches, meta changes, and strategies.

b. Establish an Online Presence:
  - Make sure you have a presence on gaming platforms and social media.
  - Share your highlights and achievements, and engage with the gaming community.

The Success You Can't See

c. Join Gaming Communities:
   - Participate in online forums, Discord channels, and social media groups.
   - Networking can open up valuable connections and opportunities.

d. Stream Your Gameplay:
   - Consider streaming your gameplay on platforms like Twitch or YouTube.
   - Streaming can help you build an audience and show off your skills.

e. Collaborate with Other Gamers:
   - Team up with other gamers for joint streams or competitions.
   - Working together can help you increase your visibility.

f. Enter Tournaments and Competitions:
   - Participate in gaming tournaments and competitions.

- Doing well in these events can attract sponsorships and recognition.

g. Stay Physically and Mentally Healthy:
- Make sure you have a balanced lifestyle with regular exercise and healthy habits.
- Physical and mental well-being are essential for sustained gaming performance.

h. Invest in Quality Gaming Equipment:
- Invest in a reliable gaming setup, including a high-performance PC, peripherals, and a stable internet connection.
- Quality equipment can make a huge difference in your gameplay and overall experience.

i. Learn from Your Mistakes:
- Analyze your gameplay and learn from your mistakes.
- Continuous improvement is key to staying competitive.

j. Stay Informed on Industry Trends:
   - Keep up with the gaming industry, trends, and upcoming releases.
   - Adapt to changes and be versatile in the games you play.

Introduction:
18. Launching an affiliate marketing business requires careful planning and execution. To make the most of this performance-based model, here are some tips to keep in mind:

a. Pick Relevant Products and Niches:
   - Choose products or services that match your interests and knowledge.
   - Focus on niches where you can provide helpful advice and recommendations.

b. Establish Trust with Your Audience:
- Build trust by being open and honest in your recommendations.
- Make sure to disclose your affiliate relationships and only promote products you truly believe in.

c. Diversify Affiliate Programs:
- Join a variety of affiliate programs to diversify your income sources.
- Look into programs with different commission structures and payment methods.

d. Generate High-Quality Content:
- Create valuable and engaging content that educates and informs.
- Use a mix of written content, videos, and visuals to appeal to different audiences.

e. Optimize for Search Engines:

- Implement SEO best practices to increase the visibility of your content.
- Target relevant keywords to attract organic traffic.

f. Utilize Social Media Strategically:
- Leverage social media platforms to promote your affiliate links.
- Build a community and engage with your audience through various channels.

g. Stay Up-to-Date on Products:
- Stay informed about product features, updates, and promotions.
- Regularly check in with affiliate programs for the latest information.

h. Track and Analyze Performance:
- Use analytics tools to track the performance of your affiliate links.

- Analyze which strategies and products are generating the most conversions.

i. Experiment with Different Promotional Tactics:
- Try out different promotional tactics, such as email marketing or webinars.
- Identify what resonates best with your audience and adjust your approach accordingly.

j. Develop Long-Term Relationships:
- Foster relationships with both your audience and affiliate program managers.
- Long-term relationships can lead to exclusive offers and increased earning potential.

To be successful as an online entrepreneur, it's important to identify a profitable niche, develop a comprehensive business plan, build a strong online presence, embrace e-commerce and digital products, cultivate a community around your brand, utilize automation tools, stay adaptable and innovative, network and collaborate, provide exceptional customer service, and manage finances effectively.

Start by choosing a niche with demand and growth potential, and focus on areas where you can provide unique value or solve a specific problem. Outline your business goals, target audience, and revenue streams, and plan for scalability and future expansion. Invest in a professional website and optimize it for search engines, and leverage social media and content marketing to broaden your online reach.

Explore e-commerce opportunities and consider selling digital products, such as online courses or ebooks, to provide scalable income.

Build a community through social media, forums, or a dedicated platform, and engage with your audience, collect feedback, and create a loyal customer base. Implement automation tools for tasks like email marketing and customer relationship management to enhance efficiency and allow you to focus on strategic aspects.

Stay informed about industry trends and technological advancements, and be willing to adapt your business model. Network with other entrepreneurs in your industry, and collaborate on projects, joint ventures, or mutually beneficial partnerships.

Prioritize excellent customer service to build a positive reputation, and happy customers will become brand advocates and contribute to business growth. Lastly, keep meticulous records of your income and expenses, and consider working with financial

professionals to optimize your
financial strategy.

Common Challenges in the Journey Toward Online Success for Young Adults

Beginning a journey to success online, especially for young adults, can be an exciting yet daunting experience. Navigating the digital world comes with its own set of obstacles. It is essential to be aware of and prepare for these challenges to build resilience and achieve long-term success. Here are some of the common issues young adults may face:

1. **Information Overload:**
   - *Challenge:* The internet is full of information, making it difficult for young adults to find the relevant and reliable content they need.
   - *Solution:* Developing critical thinking skills to identify credible sources is key. Focus on reliable

sources and prioritize quality over quantity in your learning.

2. **Balancing Online and Offline Life:**
   - *Challenge:* The line between online and offline life can become blurred, making it hard to maintain a healthy work-life balance.
   - *Solution:* Establish clear boundaries between work and leisure. Schedule dedicated offline time, take part in hobbies, and build meaningful connections outside the digital world.

3. **Digital Fatigue and Burnout:**
   - *Challenge:* Too much screen time, multitasking, and the pressure to stay connected can lead to digital fatigue and burnout.
   - *Solution:* Self-care is essential. Take regular breaks, exercise, and get enough sleep. Learn to recognize the signs of burnout and adjust your digital activities accordingly.

4. **Imposter Syndrome:**
   - *Challenge:* Young adults entering the online space may experience imposter syndrome, doubting their skills and feeling inadequate compared to others.
   - *Solution:* Remember that everyone starts somewhere. Focus on your progress, celebrate small victories, and seek mentorship or support to boost your confidence.

5. **Financial Pressures:**
   - *Challenge:* Monetizing digital skills can take time, and young adults may face financial pressures if they are relying on online ventures for income.
   - *Solution:* Create a realistic financial plan, explore multiple income streams, and consider part-time or freelance work while building your online presence.

6. **Online Security and Privacy Concerns:**

- *Challenge:* The digital world is full of cybersecurity threats, and young adults may struggle to protect their online privacy.
- *Solution:* Educate yourself on online security best practices, use secure passwords, enable two-factor authentication, and be careful about sharing personal information online.

7. **Staying Up-to-Date in a Changing Landscape:**
- *Challenge:* The digital world is constantly evolving, and it can be difficult to keep up. Young adults may worry about being left behind or becoming outdated.
- *Solution:* Adopt a growth mindset and prioritize ongoing learning. Stay informed about industry trends, engage in professional development, and be open to acquiring new skills.

8. **Dealing with Criticism and Online Feedback:**
   - *Challenge:* Online platforms can expose individuals to public feedback, including criticism. It can be emotionally tough to handle negative comments or critiques.
   - *Solution:* Build resilience and a healthy attitude toward feedback. Focus on constructive criticism for improvement, and don't let negativity derail your journey.

9. **Maintaining Consistency and Discipline:**
   - *Challenge:* Establishing a successful online presence requires consistency and discipline, which can be difficult for young adults with many responsibilities.
   - *Solution:* Create a realistic schedule, set achievable goals, and prioritize tasks. Develop habits that promote consistency, and be patient with yourself as you face challenges.

10. **Legal and Regulatory Compliance:**
   - *Challenge:* Understanding and following legal and regulatory requirements in the online space can be complex, especially for young adults starting out.
   - *Solution:* Get familiar with relevant laws and regulations, seek legal advice if needed, and make sure your online activities comply with ethical and legal standards.

11. **Time Management:**
   - *Challenge:* Balancing education, work, and personal life alongside online ventures can be a challenge when it comes to time management.
   - *Solution:* Prioritize tasks, set realistic deadlines, and use productivity tools to manage time effectively. Learn to delegate or outsource tasks when possible.

12. **Networking Difficulties:**
   - *Challenge:* Establishing a professional network online can be

difficult, especially for those who are introverted or new to the industry.

   - *Solution:* Participate actively in online communities, attend virtual events, and connect with professionals in your field. Networking is a valuable asset for career growth.

13. **Adapting to Technology Changes:**

   - *Challenge:* Rapid advancements in technology can require constant adaptation, which can be a challenge for young adults to keep up with.

   - *Solution:* Embrace a mindset of lifelong learning. Stay curious, explore emerging technologies, and be proactive in acquiring new skills as the digital landscape evolves.

14. **Handling Competition:**

   - *Challenge:* The online space is often highly competitive, and young adults may feel the pressure

to stand out among a sea of
competitors.
   - *Solution:* Focus on your
unique strengths and value
proposition. Differentiate yourself
by showcasing your authentic
voice, skills, and innovative ideas.

15. **Cultural and Linguistic
Barriers:**
   - *Challenge:* Engaging in the
global digital space may expose
young adults to cultural and
linguistic differences that can be
difficult to navigate.
   - *Solution:* Cultivate cultural
awareness, be open to diverse
perspectives, and consider
language diversity in your online
communications. This enhances
global collaboration and audience
engagement.

16. **Evolving Trends in Digital
Marketing:**
   - *Challenge:* Keeping up with
the latest trends in digital
marketing can be overwhelming, as

strategies and algorithms are always changing.

- *Solution:* Dedicate time to ongoing education, follow industry leaders, and participate in webinars or courses. Being adaptable to changes in digital marketing trends is essential for sustained success.

17. **Managing Intellectual Property:**
    - *Challenge:* Protecting intellectual property, such as original content, can be a concern in the digital space.
    - *Solution:* Learn about copyright laws, trademark regulations, and licensing agreements. Consider registering your work when applicable, and be careful about sharing sensitive content.

18. **Building a Personal Brand:**
    - *Challenge:* Establishing a recognizable personal brand takes time and strategic effort.

- *Solution:* Define your personal brand, create consistent messaging, and use various platforms to showcase your expertise. Engage authentically with your audience to build a genuine online presence.

19. **Managing Expectations:**
   - *Challenge:* Unrealistic expectations about quick success can lead to frustration and disappointment.
   - *Solution:* Set achievable short-term goals, celebrate small wins, and view challenges as learning opportunities. Building a successful online presence is a gradual process.

20.**Dealing with Technical Difficulties:**
- *Problem:* Technical problems can interfere with online activities, reducing efficiency and user satisfaction.
- *Solution:* Keep up to date on troubleshooting methods, have a

backup plan ready, and remain
patient when technical issues arise.
Additionally, staying informed
about the tools you use can help to
prevent and address technical
issues.

Overcoming Obstacles:
Strategies for Staying Resilient
in the Online Journey

Beginning an online journey can be exciting, but it's not without its difficulties. Overcoming obstacles is an essential part of the path to success, and resilience is the key to navigating these hurdles.

Here are some tips and advice to help young adults overcome obstacles and stay resilient in their pursuit of online success:

1. **Develop a Growth Mindset:**
   - *Strategy:* View challenges as opportunities for growth rather than setbacks. A growth mindset encourages resilience by seeing difficulties as a chance to learn and improve.

2. **Set Realistic Goals:**
   - *Strategy:* Establish achievable short-term and

long-term goals. Break larger objectives into smaller, more manageable tasks. Celebrate accomplishments along the way to stay motivated.

3. **Build a Support System:**
   - *Strategy:* Surround yourself with a network of supportive people, such as mentors, peers, or friends. Share your struggles and seek guidance. A supportive community can provide valuable insights and encouragement.

4. **Practice Self-Care:**
   - *Strategy:* Prioritize self-care to maintain physical and mental well-being. Establish a healthy routine that includes regular breaks, exercise, and adequate sleep. Taking care of yourself enhances resilience in the face of challenges.

5. **Learn from Failures:**
   - *Strategy:* View failures as learning experiences rather than

setbacks. Analyze what went wrong, identify lessons, and use that knowledge to improve future endeavors. Every setback is an opportunity for growth.

6. **Cultivate Adaptability:**
   - *Strategy:* The digital landscape is ever-changing, and adaptability is a valuable trait. Be open to change, stay informed about industry trends, and be willing to adjust your strategies when necessary.

7. **Break Tasks into Manageable Steps:**
   - *Strategy:* When faced with a daunting task, break it down into smaller, more achievable steps. Tackling one step at a time makes the process less overwhelming and boosts confidence.

8. **Seek Professional Development:**
   - *Strategy:* Invest in continuous learning and professional

development. Stay up-to-date on industry trends, attend webinars, and enroll in relevant courses. The more knowledge and skills you acquire, the better equipped you are to overcome challenges.

9. **Celebrate Small Wins:**
   - *Strategy:* Acknowledge and celebrate even the smallest successes. Recognizing progress, no matter how minor, reinforces a positive mindset and encourages perseverance during difficult times.

10. Build resilience
Navigating challenges can be difficult, but with the right strategies and a positive attitude, it is possible to overcome obstacles. To build resilience, incorporate mindfulness practices and stress-management techniques into your routine, such as meditation, deep breathing, or yoga.

11. Establish a financial plan and explore multiple income streams to

ensure financial stability. Develop strong communication skills to express ideas effectively, resolve conflicts, and build positive relationships.

12. Diversify your skill sets to make yourself more adaptable and marketable. Remind yourself of the reasons behind your online journey to stay motivated.

13. Embrace feedback as a tool for improvement and be willing to adjust your approach if you encounter obstacles.

14. Celebrate your uniqueness and use it to build a strong personal brand.

15. Connect with mentors who have navigated similar challenges and learn from their experiences.

16. Lastly, maintain a positive outlook and practice gratitude to enhance resilience. With these

strategies, you can stay focused and make progress towards your goals.

Ten motivating success stories
of people who have attained
financial success with the help
of their smartphones

1. **Sarah, the Freelance Writer:**
   - *Background:* Sarah, a
passionate writer, began her
freelance writing career with her
smartphone. Despite having limited
resources, she used writing apps,
editing tools, and online platforms
to offer her services.
   - *Journey:* Sarah started by
creating a profile on freelancing
websites, offering her expertise in
content creation. Gradually, she
built a client base, got positive
reviews, and increased her rates.
Her smartphone became her virtual
office, allowing her to work from
anywhere.
   - *Outcome:* Sarah turned her
love for writing into a steady

income. She now manages a team of freelance writers, growing her business and contributing articles to well-known publications.

2. **Alex, the Social Media Manager:**
   - *Background:* Alex, a social media enthusiast, used his smartphone to launch a career as a social media manager. Equipped with creative apps and scheduling tools, he began managing social media accounts for small businesses.
   - *Journey:* Alex showed off his skills by increasing the online presence of his clients. As news of his expertise spread, he expanded his clientele and started offering workshops on social media marketing.
   - *Outcome:* Now, Alex runs a successful social media management agency, helping businesses across industries boost their online visibility. His smartphone remains his primary

tool for content creation, scheduling, and client communication.

3. **Jasmine, the E-commerce Entrepreneur:**
   - *Background:* Jasmine, a young businesswoman, used her smartphone to launch an e-commerce venture. She identified a gap in the market for handmade jewelry and accessories.
   - *Journey:* Jasmine started by creating an online store with e-commerce apps. She used social media to showcase her products and communicate with customers. Her smartphone became her shop window, allowing her to manage orders and customer queries on the go.
   - *Outcome:* Jasmine's e-commerce business flourished, and she expanded her product range. Her brand gained recognition, and she now mentors other aspiring entrepreneurs in

using smartphones for online business success.

4. **Mark, the Online Educator:**
   - *Background:* Mark, an expert in digital marketing, used his knowledge to create a profitable venture by becoming an online educator.
   - *Journey:* Mark created digital courses using his smartphone, covering topics such as SEO, social media marketing, and content creation. He used platforms that catered to mobile users and promoted his courses through social media.
   - *Outcome:* Mark's courses gained popularity, attracting a global audience. His online education platform became a significant source of passive income, allowing him to focus on creating high-quality content for his students.

5. **Priya, the App Developer:**

- *Background:* Priya, with a background in coding, developed a mobile app to address a specific need in her community.
- *Journey:* Using her smartphone, Priya designed, coded, and tested her app. She used online platforms to promote the app and gather user feedback. Through continuous improvement, she enhanced the app's features.
- *Outcome:* Priya's app gained traction, solving a real-world problem. She monetized the app through in-app purchases and advertisements. Priya's success led her to collaborate with other developers and expand her portfolio of mobile applications.

6. **Carlos, the Digital Artist:**
- *Background:* Carlos, a self-taught digital artist, used his smartphone to create stunning artworks and illustrations.
- *Journey:* Carlos displayed his art on social media platforms and used smartphone apps for digital

art creation. He interacted with his audience, offering custom commissions and selling prints of his work.

- *Outcome:* Carlos built a strong online presence and monetized his art through various channels. He collaborated with brands, held virtual art exhibitions, and turned his passion into a thriving online business.

7. **Aisha, the Podcast Host:**
   - *Background:* Aisha, passionate about a particular niche, started her own podcast using only her smartphone.
   - *Journey:* Aisha researched and scripted episodes, recorded them using her smartphone's built-in microphone, and edited the content using mobile apps. She shared her podcasts on various platforms and engaged with her audience through social media.
   - *Outcome:* Aisha's podcast gained a dedicated following. She monetized her content through

sponsorships, affiliate marketing, and listener support. Aisha's success allowed her to expand her podcast and explore additional ventures within her niche.

8. **Elena, the Virtual Assistant:**
   - *Background:* Elena, a detail-oriented professional, decided to pursue a career as a virtual assistant using her smartphone.
   - *Journey:* Elena provided administrative services, managed calendars, and responded to customer inquiries using communication apps. She used productivity tools and mobile applications to manage projects, transforming her smartphone into a mobile office.
   - *Outcome:* Elena's virtual assistant business flourished as she gained clients from various industries. Her smartphone-centric approach enabled her to work

remotely and serve clients around the world, creating a flexible and profitable career.

9. **Raj, the Mobile Photographer:**
   - *Background:* Raj, with a passion for photography, used his smartphone to take and edit stunning images.
   - *Journey:* Raj built an online portfolio to showcase his smartphone photography skills. He utilized social media platforms and photography apps to reach a larger audience. His smartphone became a full-fledged photography studio, from capturing moments to editing and sharing them online.
   - *Outcome:* Raj's captivating photos gained attention, leading to collaborations with brands and media outlets. He monetized his photography through exhibitions, selling prints, and offering smartphone photography workshops.

10. **Lila, the E-book Author:**
   - *Background:* Lila, an avid reader and storyteller, used her smartphone to become a successful ebook author.
   - *Journey:* Lila wrote and self-published novels using mobile writing apps. She designed book covers, created marketing materials, and interacted with readers through social media apps on her smartphone.
   - *Outcome:* Lila's e-books gained popularity in online marketplaces. Her storytelling skills and smartphone-centric marketing strategies enabled her to build a devoted reader base. Lila's success extended beyond e-books, leading to opportunities in traditional publishing and literary collaborations.

Future Opportunities in the
Digital Space

As technology continues to evolve, the digital space is becoming increasingly dynamic, offering a wealth of opportunities for those looking to capitalize on its power. As we look to the future, several emerging trends are emerging that could lead to exciting prospects for innovation, entrepreneurship, and financial success.

One such trend is the concept of the metaverse, a virtual shared space that combines aspects of augmented reality (AR), virtual reality (VR), and the internet. This immersive digital realm provides a platform for new forms of entertainment, social interactions, and even business ventures. Entrepreneurs can take advantage of this trend by creating virtual experiences, offering virtual goods and services, and reaching audiences in innovative ways.

Another trend is the rise of blockchain technology and non-fungible tokens (NFTs). NFTs are unique digital assets verified through blockchain, providing authenticity and ownership in the digital space. This opens up opportunities for artists, musicians, and creators to monetize their digital work, as well as for entrepreneurs to explore blockchain applications for secure transactions, smart contracts, and decentralized finance.

The integration of Artificial Intelligence (AI) into various industries is also reshaping the digital space. AI-powered ventures are becoming increasingly popular, from developing AI-driven applications and chatbots to implementing AI solutions to enhance efficiency and decision-making processes. Those skilled in machine learning and data science can take advantage of this trend to explore profitable opportunities.

Finally, the emphasis on sustainability and eco-friendly practices is also transforming the tech industry. From green energy solutions to eco-conscious design, sustainable tech is becoming a major focus for innovation. Entrepreneurs can explore opportunities in this area, such as developing clean energy solutions, eco-friendly products, and sustainable tech practices. The intersection of technology and environmental responsibility offers a pathway for impactful and profitable ventures.

5G Technology Adoption:

 - *Trend:* 5G technology is revolutionizing connectivity and communication, offering faster speeds and more reliable networks. This opens up new possibilities for mobile experiences, IoT applications, and augmented reality.

 - *Opportunity:* Entrepreneurs can take advantage of 5G capabilities by creating high-speed mobile applications or innovative solutions for industries that benefit from low-latency and high-bandwidth connectivity.

Health Tech Revolution:

 - *Trend:* The combination of technology and healthcare, known as Health Tech, is undergoing a revolution. Telemedicine, wearable devices, and AI-driven diagnostics are transforming how healthcare services are delivered.
 - *Opportunity:* Entrepreneurs can explore opportunities in health tech, such as developing health monitoring apps, wearable devices, or platforms that facilitate remote

healthcare services. Technology and healthcare are merging to provide improved patient care and wellness.

Personalized Digital Experiences:

- *Trend:* Consumers are expecting tailored content, recommendations, and interactions across digital platforms.
- *Opportunity:* Entrepreneurs can capitalize on the trend of personalization by creating platforms, services, or content that caters to individual preferences. Personalized marketing, content creation, and user experiences offer businesses the chance to connect with their audiences in more meaningful ways.

Edge Computing:

- *Trend:* Edge computing, where data processing is done near the source of data generation, is becoming more popular. This reduces latency and increases the efficiency of data-intensive applications.

- *Opportunity:* Entrepreneurs can explore opportunities in edge computing by developing applications that benefit from low-latency processing. Industries such as IoT, augmented reality, and real-time analytics can take advantage of the advancements in edge computing.

Cybersecurity Innovations:

- *Trend:* With the increasing digitization of businesses and personal data, the need for cybersecurity is greater than ever. Cyber threats are constantly evolving, requiring continuous innovation in cybersecurity solutions.

- *Opportunity:* Entrepreneurs can explore opportunities in cybersecurity by developing advanced threat detection systems, secure communication tools, and innovative solutions to protect digital assets. The growing demand for robust cybersecurity measures presents a thriving market for innovative solutions.

Remote Collaboration Tools:

- *Trend:* The rise of remote work has increased the need for efficient collaboration tools. Video conferencing, project management, and communication platforms are essential for remote work setups.
- *Opportunity:* Entrepreneurs can explore opportunities in developing and improving remote collaboration tools. Innovations in virtual collaboration, team communication, and project management tools offer solutions to the changing needs of remote and distributed teams.

The Lifelong Journey to Success

In today's ever-changing digital world, knowledge is no longer a one-time pursuit; it's a lifelong commitment. Continuous learning has become a key factor in achieving personal and professional success, especially in industries that are heavily influenced by technological advancements and dynamic shifts. Here's why staying up-to-date on industry trends and acquiring new skills is essential for navigating the ever-evolving landscape:

1. **Adapting to Technological Developments:**
   - *Rapid Changes:* Technology is advancing at an unprecedented rate. Continuous learning ensures that individuals stay abreast of the latest technological developments,

allowing them to adjust their skills and strategies accordingly.

   - *Opportunity:* Embracing new technologies positions individuals as innovators rather than observers. Whether it's artificial intelligence, blockchain, or the latest programming languages, those who are committed to learning are better equipped to take advantage of emerging tools.

2. **Securing Your Career:**
   - *Shift in Job Markets:* Job markets are undergoing major changes due to automation, AI, and other technological disruptions. Continuous learning ensures professionals remain relevant, making them more resilient in the face of industry shifts.
   - *Versatility:* Developing a diverse skill set makes individuals more adaptable. It not only enhances job security but also opens doors to new opportunities and career paths, allowing for

greater flexibility in navigating a dynamic job market.

3. **Improving Problem-Solving Abilities:**
   - *Complex Challenges:* Industries today face increasingly complex challenges. Continuous learning enhances problem-solving abilities by providing individuals with the tools and knowledge needed to effectively tackle intricate issues.
   - *Critical Thinking:* Learning new concepts and methodologies fosters critical thinking skills. This, in turn, allows individuals to approach problems with fresh perspectives, leading to innovative solutions.

4. **Fostering Professional Growth and Advancement:**
   - *Career Development:* Continuous learning is synonymous with career development. It allows individuals to climb the professional ladder,

take on leadership roles, and make meaningful contributions to their respective fields.

- *Leadership Opportunities:* Those who invest in continuous learning often find themselves in leadership positions. Their ability to guide teams through change and innovation is a testament to the value of ongoing education.

5. **Achieving Entrepreneurial Success:**

- *Innovating in Business:* For entrepreneurs, staying up-to-date on market trends, consumer behavior, and emerging technologies is essential for developing and sustaining successful ventures. Continuous learning is the key to driving innovation.

- *Reducing Risk:* By educating themselves, entrepreneurs can anticipate market shifts and reduce risks. This proactive approach increases the chances of long-term success.

6. **Networking and Collaboration:**
   - *Broadening Connections:* Continuous learners often find themselves part of expansive professional networks. Participating in learning opportunities provides avenues for connecting with like-minded individuals, mentors, and collaborators.
   - *Collaborative Innovation:* In collaborative environments, the exchange of ideas and skills is essential. Continuous learners contribute to a culture of innovation, creating synergies that lead to collective success.

7. **Personal Fulfillment and Well-Being:**
   - *Intellectual Stimulation:* Learning is a source of intellectual stimulation and personal satisfaction. The pursuit of

knowledge enhances mental well-being and brings a sense of accomplishment.

  - *Adaptable Mindset:* Continuous learners develop an adaptable mindset. They view change as an opportunity for growth, leading to a positive outlook and a more resilient approach to life's challenges.

8. **Global Perspective:**

  - *Cultural Awareness:* Learning extends beyond technical skills to encompass cultural intelligence. Acquiring knowledge about diverse cultures and global trends fosters a more inclusive and informed worldview.

  - *Global Opportunities:* In an interconnected world, individuals with a global perspective are better positioned to take advantage of international opportunities, whether in business, academia, or cross-cultural collaborations.

9. **Resourcefulness in Digital Age:**

   - *Access to Information:* The digital age provides unprecedented access to information. Continuous learners take advantage of online courses, webinars, podcasts, and other digital resources to stay informed.

   - *Self-Directed Learning:* With a plethora of self-directed learning resources available, individuals can customize their educational journey to their specific needs and preferences, fostering autonomy and resourcefulness.

10. **Cultivating Curiosity and Passion:**

    - *Lifelong Curiosity:* Continuous learning encourages a lifelong curiosity for discovery and exploration. This inherent curiosity becomes a driving force for personal and professional development.

    - *Passion Pursuit:* Learning about subjects of personal interest leads to a passionate pursuit of knowledge. This passion not only increases engagement but also fuels sustained motivation in the pursuit of excellence.

Conclusion:

Empowering the Digital Journey

As you embark on your journey to make money with your smartphone, remember that every step forward, no matter how small, is a step toward your goals. The journey explored in "The Success You Can't See" has highlighted the idea that success, often hidden from plain sight, is achievable through the use of smartphone capabilities. Digital skills are essential catalysts for propelling individuals towards new possibilities, ventures, and financial independence. The invention of the smartphone has opened up a world of opportunities, from freelance writing to virtual assistance, podcasting to e-commerce. Challenges are not roadblocks but stepping stones to resilience and innovation. It is important to stay updated on industry trends, acquire new skills, and cultivate a mindset of lifelong curiosity for sustained success in the ever-changing digital landscape.

As you navigate the unseen path ahead, remember that the success you seek is not always visible to the naked eye—it is the result of your efforts, resilience, and unwavering commitment to continuous growth. So, young adventurers, go forth with confidence. The digital landscape is yours to explore, innovate within, and conquer. The success you can't see is waiting to be uncovered by the magic within your smartphone and the brilliance within you. May your journey be filled with discovery, achievement, and the realization of your fullest potential. Here's to the success that awaits you—the success you can't see, but undoubtedly, the success you will achieve.

The Success You Can't See

For more interesting books from Same Author

www.ingramcontent.com/pod-product-compliance
Lightning Source LLC
Chambersburg PA
CBHW062323290526
45794CB00005B/1874